Sing A New Song II

Christmas 2003

Rosita,
'Hope to meet you for
coffee when I come
to my class reunion
in October —
God bless 2004 for
you + all those you love!

Pat

Sing A New Song II

Patricia C. Montesano

GMA Publishing

GMA Publishing
Newburgh, Indiana

GMAPublishing.com
Check out our website
GMA is a global publishing company
Our books are available and distributed around the world and can be found on the internet at Amazon, Barnes and Noble and any major bookseller.

GMAPublishing@aol.com

With the exception of family members, all names have been changed to protect their privacy.

Cover By: Cecilia Brendel
Manuscript Assistant: John Beanblossom

Printed in the United States of America

From the beginning of life's journey for Chris, we had been told that society was changing towards those with mental retardation. We were encouraged to educate Chris, to train him to be socially acceptable, and to believe that he would someday be a contributing member of our society.

We spent large amounts of money, made great sacrifices for the effort, and gave one hundred percent of ourselves, so that Chris would become a useful citizen on earth. We were excited about his accomplishments and his eagerness to be recognized as a contributor in the community of the world.

However, when the time came, we did not find a world that welcomed Chris. What we found was discrimination, no equal opportunities, no justice. We experienced exploitation, deceit, and pain. We, as Chris's family, together with Chris, had believed he would be accepted as a neighbor, a fellow parishioner, a welcome guest at social events, a shopper, a passenger, an employee, and simply as a friend.

There have been many kind and generous people throughout Chris's life. We have not been totally disappointed in our expectations for him

Unfortunately, in reality, we found a world which promotes the eradication of unborn babies who might be born with this handicap. Hopefully, this book will help to generate more unconditional acceptance.

Pat Montesano 2002

Acknowledgements

*To **Sunsweeper Organization**, dedicated to research and change to benefit all those in the world with developmental challenges, believing in the value of each of those lives. Also, for personal interest and generosity towards the publication of this book, Thank You!*
http://sunsweeper.com

To Frank, for generosity and creative license in designing the website which tells about Sing A New Song (I and II), Thank You!   Additional thanks for editing, advertising, and promotion, as well as updating the cover of this book.

Please visit www.singanewsong.50megs.com
and http://montesanoenterprises.com

To **all my children,** for their willingness to open their hearts and reveal their personal thoughts and feelings, as part of this book, and for their encouragement and help in many ways to bring Chris's story to the readers, Thank You!

A 10% donation from the sale of each book will go to
Colorado Springs Faith and Light Community

Table of Contents

Introduction – *Sibling Reflections*

INTRODUCTION

Sibling Reflections

To Be

You know I see it in my mind,

the perfect sense of life and time.

You know I feel it in my heart,

the perfect way that life should start.

You know we're here where we belong,

amidst the waves of life's earthen shores.

You know we won't be here for long,

because we are the stars to be shown.

Frank John Montesano 2002

Thanks, Chris, for helping me appreciate the gifts God has given that I take for granted, and for helping me become more aware of inner beauty and truth.

Love you.

By Chris's brother, Frank
(2 years older than Chris)

Whenever I think of my birthday, I think of my brother, Chris, and my Dad.

The way the story goes, as my Mom was leaving for the hospital on my first birthday, she told me she was going to get me a very special birthday gift. My brother, Chris, was born that day; yes! What a great gift! We have always celebrated together with, of course, two cakes.

I recall only one birthday when we weren't able to celebrate together. Chris lived 300 miles away at a private residential school for children with mental retardation. We planned to go and get Chris and bring him home for Thanksgiving and our birthday celebration. However, I decided to take a ride in the go-cart and went at high speed towards the steep hill in our neighborhood. To save myself, I grabbed on to a neighbor's mailbox pole, and crashed. I spent time in the hospital being treated for a broken collarbone. I recall having to wear a heavy leather shoulder brace for a long time. We weren't able to get Chris until after Thanksgiving and our birthday.

The 23rd of November 1976 changed our birthday forever, though. On that day our Dad was buried, making it even more special for us.

By Chris's brother, Paul
(1 year older than Chris)

My brother, Chris's life has so much value to it! This value, to me, cannot be measured in dollar signs or earthly materials. One of his values is a very important lesson, a lesson from the Bible. It tells us that God will give us everything we need to live.

Chris's thoughtfulness towards his family is second to none. I thought I was doing well all these years by remembering all the birthdays of my brothers and sisters, my mother, my father, my wife, and my children.

Chris has recorded, in his memory, all of these **plus** *all the birthdays of his nieces and nephews, each of his sisters-in-law, brothers-in-law, as well as all of their families, and even the birthdays of his cousins. That, in itself, is a great lesson in respect!*

I could go on forever! For now, however, I will just continue to learn from my older brother, Chris, who has taught me so many lessons in life.

By Chris's brother, Mike
(18 months younger than Chris)

My brother, Chris, has taught me to appreciate things in life that we often take for granted, and which he is deprived of: a spouse, a relationship where cuddling and intimacy is experienced, the privilege of parenting, a driver's license, independence, the understanding of what others are talking about, being understood when talking...and so much more.

I appreciate having dreams come true, because I see that Chris has not had many dreams come true. It seems as though he's not allowed many dreams to dream.

By Chris's sister, Donna
(4 years younger than Chris)

How can a person with so many handicaps always be so caring, so loving, so considerate and thoughtful?

How can he always be so happy?

I wonder about my brother, Chris. I wonder how he gets up so cheerful every morning.

With all his handicaps, I wonder how he manages to be so kindhearted, talking about wishing someone "Happy Birthday," or offering to help with our laundry or take the trash out. He's so happy to say, "I prayed for you."

How can he be so good to others all the time when he's the one with the handicaps?

By Chris's sister, Patti
(6 years younger than Chris)

Chris and I shared something in our childhood: we both loved to eat cereal. I remember how he used to get up at night and eat all the cereal while sitting in the dark kitchen.

Chris likes to have fun too! I was nine years old during the second year we were living in our family home in Colorado, and our cousins came to visit that summer. My cousin, Bobby, and I thought it would be fun to fold down the baby carriage, which was stored in the garage, and use it as a vehicle to ride on. Chris wanted to be the first one, so we let him have the first try. He got on and we gave him a push, to get started down the hill. We were all laughing as he took off, until he crashed into a tree. He got up, looked up at us, brushed himself off as he laughed, and said he would try it again. He kept riding down the hill, crashing into the tree, get up laughing, and then want to try it again. I don't recall many times when I've laughed so hard! I think that's why Chris kept doing it, because he loves to see people laughing

.

I love to see him laugh too.

He just kept getting back up............

By Chris's brother, Jimmy
(8 years younger than Chris)

Chris was always the best playmate! When I was a little girl, I loved playing with him because he let me choose what we would play, and agreed with everything I wanted to do. I think we learned tolerance and patience from each other.

When Chris went off to work at Good Will I missed him terribly. One day, when he would be getting paid, he told me he would bring me a surprise.

He bought me my first horse, a rocking horse.

By Chris's sister, Rosemary
(13 years younger than Chris)

"We (modern society) have built our communities around the strong when in fact we should be building our communities around the weak."

A quotation of Mary McAleese, from Ireland's L'arche Ireland website.

CHAPTER 1

Looking Back For The Last Time

I FELT HELPLESS AS I LOOKED back at him, lying in the room at the board-and-care facility in California. I was tired and there was actual pain, heavy in my heart, as I turned to look for the last time.

There he lay, 23 years old, six feet tall, and barely 120 lbs. Heavily sedated to prevent the violent behavior he had previously displayed, his mouth looked extremely dry and cracked, and his breath smelled bad. He was unshaven, his hair was long and unruly, and it was apparent he no longer cared about anything.

"He's given up," I thought, "stopped fighting for acceptance in a world which doesn't understand him."
He was my son, brain-damaged at birth, diagnosed at the age of 18 months as "mentally retarded, hearing and speech impaired."

The cloth restrainer, which confined him now to the narrow bed, was very soiled. The worn mattress reaked of urine from previous patients, and the threadbare blanket, which barely covered his legs, had been laundered so much that it had no color to it. I thought to myself that it must have once been blue.... or maybe gray.

As I watched, he began rolling his head from side to side continuously, while humming in a loud monotone. His eyes were glazed and fixed upward as he rolled his head back and forth to a fast rhythm.

"Goodbye, Chris," I called from the doorway. He stopped for a brief second without acknowledging my presence, and then resumed humming. I wanted to say, "I love you," but the lump in my throat hurt too much. I turned and walked slowly through the hall and out of the building.

I was leaving him, having run out of ways to motivate him, ways to encourage him to persevere despite ever-present obstacles. I had become frustrated in my efforts to prove to him that he was born to be an acceptable functioning member of the world. Tired of my lonely mission, I felt discouraged and exhausted. I felt as though I had no tears left to cry as I walked through the parking lot to my car.

There was nowhere else to take him on our limited budget. He had lived in private institutions from the age of 7 until he progressed into private schools for children with mental challenges, and then into residential homes for the semi-independent. He had come back home when he was 15, to live with our family. After his Dad died, a few years later, I found it necessary to place him in a nearby residential program, realizing that he was in the pain of grieving for his Dad, as were all my children. Each one grieved in a different way, mourning and missing their father. Always unhappy and defeated, Chris was constantly moving from one program to another.

His most recent violent and destructive behavior had resulted in his being admitted to the nursing facility where he now lay, incoherent.

My youngest son, Jimmy, suggested that his brother, Chris, had been lashing out at the whole world for the hurt he was feeling.

"I think that when Chris is in his 40's," Jimmy once told me, "he'll be o.k. I think he'll be normal then."

I wondered, what would "normal" be?

He had been placed in this facility by authorities while we, his family, felt helpless and sad. I had explored all options. All I could do was leave him.

I left him there in California with his two oldest brothers living nearby. I returned to Colorado to raise my younger children, who ranged in age from 9 to 16.

Unable to accept seeing Chris in a lethargic and incoherent state at the nursing home my sons called me often to complain about the conditions. They began taking him out on daily passes whenever possible.

"Mom, he can't remember anything!" Frank and Paul worried. Chris's memory had always been exceptional in certain ways. Once he met a person and asked their middle name and birthday, he never forgot that information. His brothers were now concerned about his memory loss.

Sometimes, when they let his medications wear off, Chris begged them to take him out of there. He promised to be good and do whatever he was supposed to do. It was heart wrenching for his brothers when he was pleading for their help. Unable to satisfy his cries, it became more and more difficult for them to return him to the facility after visits.

It wasn't long before my oldest son, Frank, insisted we could not abandon Chris, not leave him in the nursing facility. We began discussing the few possibilities we could think of, and wondered if we should make one more attempt to help him find his place in the world, a place where he could work and live. It seemed to us that he was entitled to some freedom in life, somehow, somewhere. Should we even dare to hope once more? Should we try again to find some happiness for him? Should we try again because he was willing to?

Chris's collect calls from the nursing home to his brothers became more frequent and more urgent sounding. He was often sobbing and pleading for their help. Then they wouldn't hear from him for several days, so they would call or drive there, and find him heavily sedated.

Finally, with the help of his brothers, Chris was released from the facility, and he flew back to Colorado with Frank, who had sold his car to buy two plane tickets. We considered it our last attempt to search for happiness and success for Chris, and worked out a plan with a physician to gradually discontinue the sedatives he had been taking.

As Chris's memory seemed to return to its original ability, all he wanted to do was to work, to be like his brothers and sisters, to pay his own bills. His Social Security check was barely enough for his survival, so he needed additional income. We were led to a successful community program managed by the state. There were interviews with Chris, Frank, and me, followed by physical and psychological examinations, and extensive planning before we were introduced to Chris's first caseworker, and he was accepted into the program.

At this time, while Frank and Chris resided with their sister, Donna and her husband, Chris needed constant reminding of the need for good hygiene and neat appearance. With daily prompting, he tried to comply, appearing every morning after shaving, with nicks and scratches from the razor. Slowly, though, there was progress resulting from constant reminders and assistance from his siblings.

His appetite was enormous, and he began eating his sister and brother-in-law "out of house and home." When he was left alone at all, he found it hard to control his eating, and ate unbelievable amounts of food.

He often let the dog out, despite being told it was an "inside dog." The police or dogcatcher would then either bring the animal to the door, or call for the dog to be picked up from the humane society's shelter, for a fee.

The household was in turmoil when Frank decided that he and Chris were ready to rent their own place. After searching through the want ads for something suitable and affordable, Frank rented a trailer in a trailer park not far from the sheltered workshop where Chris would be re-entering the work environment.

Chris was very excited about rooming with Frank, especially when the trailer turned out to be bright pink.

CHAPTER 2.

Life In A Pink Trailer

"WHAT THE.....?"

FRANK AWOKE TO COLD WATER dripping on his face, from the ceiling of the pink trailer. He jumped up quickly from the couch, soaking wet and shivering. He had given the only bedroom to Chris, and was now the victim of one of Colorado's occasional early morning rainstorms. As he hurried to put a bucket on the couch to catch the steady drip, he grabbed for a flannel shirt from the small closet the two brothers were sharing. He noticed that Chris's bed was empty. The clock read 5:00 A.M. That couldn't be right. He put his glasses on and looked again. It was 5:00 A.M.

"Where's Chris?" he thought.

Making his way through the small trailer, Frank kept calling out for his brother. He opened the front door thinking there was no reason for Chris to be outside, but he certainly wasn't inside. He shouted Chris's name into the wind and rain of the gray morning. The next-door neighbor slammed his window down, mumbling something about trying to get some sleep.

Grabbing his car keys after dressing quickly, Frank noticed the few dollars he had left on the table were gone. Of course the old Fiat wouldn't start, so Frank threw up the hood and jiggled the battery wires and hammered on the old battery. Getting back into the driver's seat he noticed his new 10-speed bike leaning, crumpled, against the trailer.

"How did that happen?" he wondered.

When the car finally started, he drove through the trailer park searching frantically for Chris. He knew he couldn't have left for his bus yet, because the bus didn't come until 7:30 a.m., to get him to his job at the workshop by 8:00 a.m. The rain was beating against the windshield, as one wiper dragged the other wiper back and forth, squeaking. (Frank had tied them together when the one stopped working.) He kept wiping the inside of the windshield which was steaming up, with his shirtsleeve, as he strained to see out. He drove past the bus stop, but no one was there.

"Where could he be?" he thought as he shivered from the cold.

He hurried into a parking space in front of the Donut Shop and ran inside for a cup of coffee-to-go.

"Hi, Frank!" Chris called from the stool where he sat eating a jelly donut and drinking a cup of coffee.

"This is my friend Bobby!"

Bobby smiled broadly, the jelly from his donut outlining his mouth.

"Hi. We're gettin' ready to go to work."

Frank joined them and tried to explain that they were out too early. This habit of rising before Frank continued daily, however, regardless of Frank's efforts to train Chris to wait until the alarm went off. Chris would hurry out to meet his friends at the bus stop or Donut Shop.

After a few weeks on the job, Chris's caseworker reported that he was doing well at the workshop, and the staff was attempting to teach him basic skills for holding a job in the firewood division. He was part of a crew which went to designated areas of the forests in the mountains, stacked firewood into a truck, and then helped to deliver it. At one of the many meetings between Frank, Chris, and the staff, however, there were complaints of Chris's shabby appearance when he arrived at the workshop each day. He wasn't brushing his teeth, shaving, or even combing his hair. So Frank and the staff agreed upon a new routine.

Chris would not rise before the alarm went off. Then he would shower, shave, and eat breakfast before making his bed. He would leave for the bus stop 10 minutes before the bus was due. Chris also agreed to pay for the repairs on the 10-speed which he had damaged by attempting to ride it when Frank wasn't home one day.

The new routine gradually took effect, and mornings started out more peacefully. Slowly, Chris also learned how to assist with grocery shopping by the two brothers going to the store together. He learned how to use a can opener, make a sandwich, heat soup, and fry hamburgers, hot dogs, and eggs. They took turns cooking for each other, and ate many failed attempts, including the various grades of partly cooked spaghetti, as Chris learned how to prepare that.

Breakfast was easy, usually cold cereal and toast, juice and coffee. Chris learned to make his own lunch to take to work, leaving dinner as the big project of each day. Frank was determined to teach Chris to prepare a few different meals.

They also opened a joint bank account, which worked out only when Frank got to Chris before he cashed his paycheck and treated all his friends to pizza. He loved to spend his earnings on his friends, but couldn't stand the disappointment of having no money for the rest of the week. He slowly learned how to budget.

Frank's Fiat wasn't running good, so he and Chris often had to push it to get it started, jumping in once it got going. Chris often ended up running behind the car, while Frank drove slow enough to allow him to jump in. Once the winter snows came, along with ice, the feat became more of a challenge for them.

Chris had never been alone at night. One evening I drove to the trailer to see how my sons were doing, and found Chris there alone. He was outside, instructing the park manager how to repair the toilet and the plumbing, which was all backed up. The manager patiently told him he would return the following day at two o'clock to make repairs, and asked Chris to be there to let him in. I was impressed with how Chris handled the conversation. Then he told me Frank had gone to the mountains overnight.

"WHAT?"

I panicked! How could Frank have left him alone? How did he know that Chris would be all right? Why had he taken such a chance? I became so upset that my 12-year old daughter, Rosemary, assured me that Chris was fine and nothing would happen. She surprised me with her confidence in him as she calmed me down.

"He's almost 25, Mom. He's o.k."

I didn't sleep well that night as my imagination went wild. I thought of all the things that could be happening.

Suppose he went out during the night?

What if a stranger went to his door?

Would he know what to do in an emergency?

What if there was a fire?

What if he got scared?

I drove to the trailer the first thing the following morning, after a distressful night. I looked in through the window and saw a perfectly clean trailer. Chris had apparently left for work. On the door was taped a note in Chris's handwriting, "Be back 2."

Chris went to work, the toilet and plumbing got repaired, and the trailer was kept clean while Frank was gone overnight. Why had I been so anxious?

After that, I noticed that things seemed to be getting better, slowly, at the trailer and the workshop. One Friday evening, however, Frank returned home after a day of work. He entered to find several of his friends sitting there with Chris. The stereo was at full blast! More of Frank's friends arrived, and the trailer began getting crowded. Some friends sat on the couch and few chairs, while others stood around, inside and out. Frank was apologizing that he had only 1 beer in the refrigerator, and no "munchies." As the crowd grew larger and larger, Frank grew suspicious. He called Chris into the small bedroom and closed the door.

"What are all these people doing here?" he demanded.

"I donno, Frank." He looked down as he shrugged his shoulders.

Frank persisted asking the same question over and over, getting the same answer, until finally Chris admitted to having called them all to come to a party that he and Frank were throwing. Frank, quietly and patiently, explained to Chris exactly why he would be going back out to apologize and explain to everyone that there was no party. There were raised eyebrows, muffled laughter, and statements of understanding to the brothers as everyone left very quickly. Chris learned to tell Frank when he felt like having company.

It wasn't long after that when Chris told Frank he didn't like his job any more. Frank encouraged him to continue until something better happened Chris agreed to keep working, but let his boss know he wasn't happy.

Eventually earning a promotion, he moved from the firewood division to the wire-stripping division. This job was somewhat more focused on detail and required much more self-discipline. His caseworker, Cliff, reported that he was doing well and appeared to catch on and to like the work. Cliff also reported that Chris seemed to be comfortable with him as his caseworker.

One evening Frank came home to find 2 new boarders at the trailer. Chris had met Bob and his friend at the bus terminal, and they told him they had nowhere to live, so Chris had invited them to come home with him. Bob assured Frank they would only stay overnight, if they could just get a good night's sleep in a warm place, out of the snowstorm. Frank agreed, and he and Chris prepared dinner for 4 that evening.

And the next evening....

And the next....

And....

Bob's friend eventually left, but Bob stayed on. He didn't mind sleeping in a sleeping bag on the floor. Bob and Chris got along well, and Frank could date the girl he had met in the meantime. Often Frank would end up sleeping on the floor, because Bob would take the couch while Frank was out on a date. Frank began to encourage Bob to be on his way since he wasn't looking for a job. Suddenly things began disappearing from the trailer, and Frank and Chris weren't willing or able to support Bob, so they told him to leave.

Chris had a difficult time dealing with the idea that Frank had a girlfriend. Frank attempted to include Chris in the relationship, but it wasn't working. There had been a time when Chris had talked of marriage for himself, but we didn't encourage that idea because we knew he wasn't able to handle emergencies or the demands of such a relationship. It seemed that he had let go of the idea as time passed, but he had a difficult time accepting Frank's having another relationship.

It wasn't long before he asked Cliff to help him find a new place to live, and it was agreed that he could move into a group home where he might be happier. Frank helped Chris ease into the new living arrangement, not far from all of us. He was excited and hopeful as he usually was when moving into a new situation. He took a new TV with him which his younger brother, Mike, had purchased for him.

Frank worried about Chris moving, but caseworkers and family suggested Chris seemed ready and anxious to have his own place. The group home was close to a bus stop, so he could commute to his job and home again. He would have plenty of company between coworkers and the other residents at the group home.

I convinced myself that this would be a safe and friendly home for my son.

CHAPTER 3.

"Why Did God Make Chris Handicapped?"

"I JUST CALLED THE COPS!"

THE LOUD MALE VOICE ON the phone startled me when I answered.

"Your son just hit me with a baseball bat and I'm having him arrested!"

This person was obviously upset. I had just returned from work and was preparing supper for my children. I attempted to ask what the problem was, but the man was shouting over and over, breathlessly, "I'm having him arrested!"

"Who are you?" I shouted over his voice.

"I'm having him arrested!" Then the person hung up.

I quickly hung up, left the kids eating, and drove to the group home, which was actually more of a boarding house, with clients who had mental challenges, each having their own bedroom. By the time I arrived, everyone had been calmed down by two police officers. The man in charge had told Chris that he had one week to move out, because he had hit the cook. Chris tearfully told me that the cook always gave him trouble.

I went back home and called my grown children to ask their opinions about what to do next. We all decided to see what solution Chris, himself, came up with.

Three days later, Chris informed me that he and his counselors had decided he should move into another group home, which actually was owned by the same person as the one he had been living in. I asked him how he would move his belongings, and he told me that his workshop boss, Clyde, would be moving him with his pickup truck.

After he was moved in I went to the address I had been given to visit Chris. This house was very run down, and it appeared there was not much supervision for the handicapped boarders. Chris had been assigned to a backyard shed to share with another client. Chris was happy because his roommate had agreed to let him share his phone. He and his roommate discovered how to call long-distance, as well as how to call collect, to friends, relatives, and friends of Chris's family members. His other pastime appeared to be standing outside the house, which was on a main street through the city, waving to everyone he knew passing by. Even though he appeared to be happy, I felt sad whenever I heard about that.

It was at this time that he was promoted out of the sheltered workshop and into a job as kitchen aide in a local restaurant. He seemed o.k. with the job, and the reports from the counselors and staff were good…. at first. However, he soon began expressing restlessness and dissatisfaction, although Clyde and the others working with Chris tried to encourage him to stay because he was doing well. He had to work a short night shift, though, which caused difficulty finding people to drive him to work and home again. His growing unhappiness with living at the boarding house surfaced at the same time.

He was advised by his caseworker and job coach that there would be no change in jobs, but he might be able to find a more suitable living arrangement if he would be patient. Frank was always called in on decisions, at Chris's request. Frank had fallen in love and was involved in his personal relationship, but never lost daily contact with Chris.

As Chris grew impatient waiting for a new home, his sister, Donna, offered to take him to live with her while she was going through a divorce. Donna and Chris were roommates for a brief period, along with her dog, Butch. This arrangement worked until Paul, Chris's older brother, invited Chris to come for a visit in California. That sounded like a wonderful opportunity, especially while waiting for a new place to live.

Paul's wife made arrangements for Chris's air travel, and we gave him the responsibility of getting time off from his restaurant job, to take a vacation. Frank drove Chris to the airport, assured him there would be better living arrangements upon his

18

return, and saw him off on his trip. He was comfortable with air travel, because he had often flown between New York City and Boston when he was enrolled in residential schools in Boston and Rhode Island as an adolescent. For this vacation flight he was placed in the care of the flight attendants until Paul met him at the airport in Los Angeles.

A few days later, I received a call from Chris's boss at the restaurant. He asked me to come in for a "badly-needed meeting." So, I went to see him the following day, and he became quite enraged during the conversation we had.

"I send him to polish the doorknobs of the entrance doors with expensive brass polish. The next thing I know a customer slips and falls on the polish he has spilled all over the floor!"

I said I was sorry about that.

"Then I see brass polish smeared all over the windows of the doors. What is that? He thinks he's cleaning the windows too?" He was getting breathless as he grew irate. "Cleaning windows with brass polish?"

I became very uneasy.

"Did you call his Job Coach about this?"

Acting as though he hadn't heard me, he continued.

"I send him upstairs to the storeroom to get something, and 2 hours later he returns with something else that I never sent him for. What's that?"

I didn't know what to say.

"I've put him on probation, but he doesn't even seem to know what I'm talking about."

I started to explain Chris's hearing problem, how he gets confused when he doesn't hear correctly, but I was quickly interrupted.

"The only reason I called you in here is to let you know what happened here. I sure hope he's happy with his new wife."

I was startled and confused.

"What do you mean? Chris has no wife."

"Well, he does now. He quit here and went to California to get married. That's what he told me."

I smiled and said that he had gone to visit his brother and his wife.

"Oh, really? Is that who he's opening up his new restaurant with?"

"New restaurant?" I gulped.

"Well, that's what he told me," the boss blurted out, "yup, going to California to open his own restaurant and doesn't need this job any more."

"So he quit?" I asked.

"You didn't know?" He scoffed. "He told me you were helping him get to California."

"Excuse me," I held my hand up to interrupt him.

"You are aware that Chris is handicapped and came to you through a job coach?"

"Yeah, yeah, whatever..." he mumbled. "Tell me about it."

"Well, I'm trying to," I offered.

"Know what? I'm not interested," he shouted before turning to walk away, slamming a chair into a table.

I made my departure as quick as possible.

Driving home I thought about Chris at this job.

How confused he must have felt, not understanding what he was sent for, guessing and hoping he had chosen the right thing to bring to the boss.

What a terrible 2 hours it must have been for him as he tried to figure it out.

Saying that he was getting married didn't sound like something Chris would say. I wondered if this boss had misunderstood him, as so often happened in Chris's statements to others.

I felt relieved for him that he had quit this job.

When I was relating this story to one of my daughters that evening, she asked the question my children had often asked: "Why do you think God made Chris handicapped anyway?"

I explained to her what I had told the others.

"I don't believe God did make Chris handicapped. I believe the doctor who delivered him made him handicapped. During Chris's birth, the umbilical cord was very short and wrapped around his neck. For several hours he was trying to be born but it was impossible because the cord was way too short. The doctor finally decided the best way to deliver Chris was to cut the cord while he was struggling to be born. From that moment until the moment he was delivered, he went without oxygen. He was very, very dark purple and was rushed to an incubator, where he was not expected to live. He was a big boy and fought to stay alive, and survived. We learned many years later, through medical testing and imaging, that his brain had been damaged during that time without oxygen."

Of course, later on I wondered why the doctor had not delivered Chris by C-section. I was not able to ask the doctor that question, though, because he committed suicide shortly after Chris's birth. I believe that God gives each of us a free will to make decisions; and I believe the doctor made a bad decision during Chris's birth.

It was the first of many times when Chris would be the victim of circumstances, the victim of someone else's decision.

CHAPTER 4.

Abuse

"Welcome back!"

FRANK GREETED CHRIS AS HE returned from his California vacation with a nice tan. He seemed immediately relieved to learn that Frank had moved his belongings into the home he shared with his wife and newborn son, Frankie. He had been able to get Chris hired at a lumberyard through the Hire The Handicapped Program. The boss agreed to give Chris a try at being a yard worker, only because Frank was employed there.

Right from the start there were problems because Chris resented being expected to stay in one place and stack lumber in proper bins. His interest was in socializing with the other employees. He was excited about working with all the men.

"HEY! WATCH OUT!"

Chris paid no attention. Although his hearing aids magnified all noise, he couldn't hear one specific noise or voice over other sounds.

He was often in the way of the forklifts and trucks as they backed up, unaware of the shouts and warnings of other workers, as one close call after another tried the patience of the busy employees.

At home Chris still didn't understand Frank's relationship with his wife. He had a hard time sharing Frank's attention. Frank's wife attempted to teach Chris how to cook, do laundry, and keep his room neat and clean. She had a 4-year old son whom Chris tattled on and accused of having eaten the missing cookies or potato chips. Meanwhile the 4-year old tattled on Chris and said he was the one who had eaten the missing food. They fought over what to watch on TV and about doing chores. Sometimes they slapped each other in passing as the situation grew tense, and the atmosphere became frustrating. Frank and his wife didn't know what to do.

Then Chris got laid off from the lumberyard, and he had to stay at home all the time. While Frank and his wife were gone to their jobs, he became restless and impatient, waiting for a new job to be found for him.

One night, when Frank was trying to promote peace and tranquility in the household, Chris exploded. He was unable to control his temper and the results were disastrous. Frank called me as he was leaving with Chris for the emergency room at the mental health facility. I met them there as Chris's anger subsided into quiet depression. He was crying as various counselors spent time talking with him, trying to console him. Upon the arrival of a psychologist, we were told that each of us would have private time to talk to him. I was the last to talk to the psychologist, and he was totally sympathetic to Chris, and advised that we move him as soon as possible into living quarters outside our family environment. He strongly suggested that Chris be moved to a group home as soon as possible.

It took weeks to get Chris enrolled in a program which promoted independent living for adults who have developmental disabilities. He became a candidate for this new program in our city, and was eager to move into a large proposed house, where he would have two roommates.

Chris and I met with Jane, a cerebral palsy victim, who was the owner of the housing-for-handicapped business. She explained that her own handicap helped her to understand the needs of other handicapped people, creating a special bond with them as she empathized with their hardships and knew their sensitivities. She quickly accepted Chris as her first client and wanted him to move in as soon as she found another client.

Chris was impatient waiting to move into his new home. It wasn't long before he was introduced to his new roommate, Donald, who functioned at the same level as Chris and suffered from cerebral palsy. We met for lunch where they made plans to move in together, while a third candidate was being sought to room with them and share expenses. Donald worked at the local YMCA, and Chris was being trained at a new sheltered workshop.

The day finally arrived when Chris happily moved into his new home where he had his own bedroom, and where Jane would visit daily to supervise housecleaning and menus for daily meals to be prepared by the young men. We were told at that time that Jane had also hired a male counselor who would make daily visits to the roommates and help them with any questions or problems that might arise. His name was Ron, and he was highly qualified and experienced in this field, according to Jane.

The old house was very large and well kept. Attractively decorated and furnished, it appealed to the young men as their secure and safe new home. Chris's brothers and sisters all expressed optimism about such an ideal home for him.

It wasn't long, however, before Chris began calling me to complain of problems with Jane and Ron. He said Jane often "popped" into his room unannounced and unexpected. While he was showering, he was embarrassed by her walking in, without knocking first, to check on him and demand that he let her wash him. She entered his room, unexpectedly, while he was sleeping.

"Mom, more problems," he lamented when he called me at my job.

He claimed that Jane was taking all of his money and not giving him an allowance, as she had agreed to do. He complained that he and Donald were afraid of Ron who often pushed them around and hurt them. When I confronted Jane about these problems, she laughed and said Chris was telling stories. Chris was adjusting to a new situation and had often had difficulty, in the past, doing so. I decided to be patient on his behalf and wait while observing the situation for a while. I assured him he was in good hands and had to be cooperative.

"Mom, it's not working out," he complained.

His phone calls continued as his fears increased. I was tired of his trying to manipulate me every time he entered a new situation. I kept telling him to be patient and to work with Jane and Ron to make the living arrangement work. He kept agreeing with me that he would try...but the phone calls continued.

"Mom, there's big problems here."

I finally got so annoyed with these phone calls that I attempted to look into the circumstances closely, so I could point out to Chris that his worries were unfounded.

I was completely shocked to discover that, indeed, Ron had bullied Donald and Chris on several occasions, had pushed both young men around, and physically abused them. When Chris had tried to complain to Jane about Ron's abuse, she refused to believe it and accused Chris of lying. She treated him abusively herself. She had restricted him to his bed for three days without use of the telephone. She ordered his roommate to report to her if Chris left his room during the three days. Both young men were frightened, and followed her orders. Donald had also been ordered, on several occasions, to sit on a chair opposite Chris and to reprimand him. Donald told me he got physically ill, sick to his stomach from those ordeals. I found out Jane had actually taken every paycheck from the boys after they endorsed them over to her. They weren't given any spending money at all. They were told they couldn't be trusted. They were ridiculed and humiliated by these people, and punished excessively.

By the time I went to complain to the state authorities who had recommended this housing facility to us, I was concerned about Chris's vulnerability and victimization. They couldn't believe what I was telling them and agreed to investigate immediately. They were as discreet as possible for the safety of the young roommates. Sure enough, they discovered Chris had been telling the truth all along. Their thorough investigation resulted in the advice that Chris be moved immediately to other quarters, while he was put under the care of a psychiatrist to help him recover from the abusive experience. I had contacted Donald's caseworker and he was treated in a similar way.

Chris and I appeared before the Board of Directors to testify about the complaints against Jane and her company. Chris was very nervous and afraid to talk about his experience. He kept asking me if Jane was coming to the Board meeting too. I had to keep reassuring him that she wouldn't come near him any more, and that he had done a good thing by telling about Jane and Ron and their abusive behavior. It was discovered that she had never conducted this business in any other states as she had reported and that, in fact, she was not qualified to operate such a business. The matter would be put into the hands of a state attorney and handled out of court, to avoid any more trauma for Chris and Donald. I knew that Chris would be traumatized if he had to tell his story in a courtroom, or was subjected to any further questioning. The end result was that no clients would be referred to Jane's company by agencies of the city; and she would eventually be out of business. Chris and I agreed to keep the whole incident confidential.

Chris moved into a small apartment by himself at his own request, under the supervision of our family. He had lost all trust in residential companies.

"Mom, you like my new cat?" He stood in the doorway of his new apartment, holding a striped kitten.

He had been given a small kitten named Sam, and they soon became buddies. He liked the apartment complex manager and often talked of how kind the man was to him. We stopped by daily and made sure Chris had a telephone installed so he could call us.

He then was offered a job as a dishwasher in the kitchen of a large international computer parts company. He accepted the job, under the supervision of a job coach who would work closely with him to help him adjust to the new work environment. He was happy to have an opportunity to work away from the workshop, and glad to be offered work for 25 hours per week. It was an excellent opportunity for him, and he surprisingly seemed to understand what he was told about future benefits which would become available to him, and how progression would occur according to a work plan. He was excited about the new steel-toed work shoes he was required to wear, purchased by the company.

It wasn't long before it seemed Chris would stick with this job and perhaps find a future for himself as a kitchen worker. He commuted back and forth by city busses and ate his lunch at work each day. He was happy with this job!

As the months went by, however, Chris seemed to be growing more and more unhappy. When we noticed him proudly wearing a new gold necklace, we questioned him about it and found out the apartment manager had bought it for him. Next we saw him wearing a new gold watch, which he said the manager had given him. Then Chris began talking about another new friend, Walt. He and Walt liked to visit each other's apartments.

As Walt and Chris became friends we heard less about the apartment manager. Then, suddenly, the phone company shut off Chris's phone, for non-payment of the bill. We discovered it had been run up to almost $700 in one month! The bill included mostly 1-900 calls which it turned out Walt had introduced Chris to: a call-for-sex number. We told him he would not be able to have a phone until he paid his previous bill. (It would take years!) We hoped, at the same time, that he had learned that he couldn't be so desperate for friends that he would allow himself to be taken advantage of. He actually seemed relieved to be moved away from the apartment manager and into another apartment complex. He and Walt were warned to stay away from each other. Walt was a client in another agency that would monitor him.

In the meantime, though, Chris had lost his job by not showing up for work for one week when he and Walt had stayed at Walt's apartment. He had been at the job for one year, had done well, and would have had gradual progression. I questioned why the job coach had not notified me when Chris wasn't showing up, but was told "we're so overloaded with cases that we can't be everywhere at all times."

Now Chris had no job and no money. His Social Security disability check covered the rent but nothing else. He was very discouraged but turned to state agencies for help. Our family pulled back to see what he would do to help himself. When he was without food, he called us for help, but we suggested he call his counselors. They showed him how to apply for food stamps and government assistance while they tried to find him another job. He learned where to go for help, and also, how limited he was without a job.

He managed to use pay phones to call the people he needed to. He took his food stamps to the grocery store and bought what he needed with some help from store employees. He pestered his counselors to hurry and find him another job, "one with 40 hours a week." He didn't want any more part time jobs. He wanted fair wages and independent living. He showed more determination to defend himself and to think of goals. This happened gradually, but it was good to know that Chris was speaking out for himself and thinking of a possible future beyond what he had previously known.

Caseworkers and job coaches had discouraged him. He felt disillusioned by some bosses and landlords. He felt mistreated, but he was ready to try again. He knew he didn't want part-time work or part-time pay, and he wanted to work for fair wages.

CHAPTER 5.

Always In Third Grade

"IN THE HOSPITAL!"

"*WHAT DO YOU MEAN HE'S IN* the hospital? What's wrong? What happened?"

I was panic-stricken! My son, Paul, had just called me to tell me Chris was in the hospital.

He had gone with a handicapped friend to cash their small paychecks and go out for pizza. On their way to the pizza parlor, they had walked into a topless bar and spent the afternoon sitting on barstools, enjoying the dancers and some beer. They stayed until they were almost out of money, after midnight. As Chris stepped off the barstool where he had been sitting for almost 12 hours, his legs folded and he fell. He laughed as his friend helped him up and outside, but Chris's legs kept folding and he kept falling. His friend decided Chris needed to go to the hospital, and hailed a cab for him. Chris went off in the cab to the emergency room, where he signed himself in for observation.

The next day, after receiving the phone call from Paul, I rushed to Chris's hospital room, and found him lounging in a hospital bed, propped up on the pillows eating a huge cheeseburger, and watching TV.

"Hi, Mom," he smilingly greeted me.

"I hurt my legs."

He complained to me about his legs and told me he had fallen off a chair at home. (I had learned the true story from his brothers.) The nurses informed me that my son was doing just fine, had shown his Medicare card in the emergency room, and given enough information to be admitted for testing.

Since my sons had explained to me what had actually happened, I told the physician, who laughed heartily before releasing Chris from the hospital, with advice to rest his legs.

Soon afterward, Chris and another handicapped friend somehow completed an application for a VISA card for Chris. You can imagine my surprise when Chris and his brother, Frank, came to show me the card, which had arrived in the mail with a $3,000 limit! Chris and his friend had even won a trip to Las Vegas for signing up. What a time I had canceling the trip and the card!

Chris is actually not legally bound by his signature, because he has a legal guardian, due to his handicap. I had to hire an attorney to release Chris from the responsibilities associated with the credit card company. The original application had been signed by Chris, stating that his annual income was $30,000.

In his need for friends Chris has given away many gifts, including a leather jacket, a new TV his brother, Mike, had given him, his bed which had belonged to his grandmother, his watch, his gold necklace, and many other belongings. Chris is naturally generous and kind, so these characteristics can easily be played upon by anyone wanting to take advantage of him. He would also use those characteristics for his own advantage, driven by his yearning for friendship.

Another bad experience helped to teach Chris about alcohol abuse, a problem we were unaware of among adults with developmental disabilities, until he was rushed to the emergency room by his sister, Patti, who had found him in an incoherent state one morning. He was treated by a neurologist who questioned me about his drinking habits because he definitely had had an alcohol-induced seizure. This would be caused, she explained, by refraining from drinking after a drinking bout; especially when previous brain damage was involved.

"Alcohol and brain damage can be a fatal combination," she warned.

We did some investigating and discovered that Chris and his friends had learned they could show their ID's and then purchase liquor at a nearby liquor store.

"We drink 'til we pass out!" one of Chris's friends told us proudly

"We buy our own booz!" boasted another with a broad grin.

"We drink whiskey!" added a young woman who had both physical and developmental difficulties.

"That's our favorite."

"Do your counselors know about this?" My kids asked.

"Sometimes," the young woman replied.

"Most of the time, we keep it secret."

Incidents like this made it difficult for me to proceed in letting go, as Chris's counselors had been advising me. Wanting to protect Chris was a high priority for me. Giving him independence was very difficult. I was torn between longing to give him independence, and feeling the need to be his protector. Feelings of guilt arose in me whenever these situations occurred.

My daughter, Patti, moved into his apartment to stay until he moved.

He asked us to move him closer to the rest of the family, so we moved him into a little cottage in town. Soon afterward, he got a new job as dishwasher in an Italian restaurant. He was especially pleased because it was his first job working 40 hours each week. I wondered about him lifting heavy trays and working in the heat and humidity. How would he get home at night? The counselors and my kids convinced me that I was worrying for no reason, that he would be safe.

There came a time, though, when the counselors did complain about the condition of Chris's new cottage.

"Terrible!" they reported after a visit.

I had a talk with Chris about it, and we agreed that he could now afford to hire someone to clean his home since he didn't want to. He understood that part of his earnings would have to be used to pay such a person, and a large part of each paycheck would go to pay his job coach for services rendered. He insisted he understood, and wanted a cleaning lady.

Chris and I interviewed different people, and he decided to hire Rita, a single Mom who needed the work. She assured us she would bring her own cleaning equipment and clean the 2-room house for $7.00 per hour. At first it would take 4 hours per week until the heavy cleaning was accomplished. The arrangements were that Chris would leave the door unlocked on Thursdays when he left for work, and he would put the estimated amount, in a money order, on the table for her. At first everything went perfectly. It was great! Chris was happy. Rita was happy. The counselors were happy. I was happy.

Then I began getting phone calls from Rita.

"The door was locked, and I couldn't get in."

I went to see Chris, to reinforce the agreement to leave the door unlocked on Thursdays. For 2 weeks he did leave the door unlocked for Rita. Then came another phone call.

"I got in but there was no money order on the table, so I didn't clean."

Rita began sounding upset. Even though I had talks with Chris about it, the problems increased. Finally I had to tell Rita not to show up until I called her. Chris then avoided me, so I went to his job to find him. He admitted that he didn't want to pay Rita any more, because he needed his money. He told his counselors and me that he would now keep his own home clean. As with anyone working full time, he found it difficult to clean the place during his time off. As the place got worse and worse, he refused to let anyone in.

His brothers tried to help him keep the small yard raked and mowed, but the little house began looking bad. Window blinds were missing slats, the metal shower got very rusty, and many fixtures were broken. When I asked the landlord to do some repairs, he responded that he charged low rent, so didn't do repairs.

Without anyone's knowledge, Chris allowed a homeless couple to move in with him. Now there were 3 tenants, plus Sam the cat, plus another gift to Chris: Sam the dog. No one cleaned. The couple didn't work, and shared Chris's food and furnishings. The told Chris they got their money by donating their blood at a local blood plasma center. They then invited a friend of theirs to move in also, along with his girlfriend.

Now there were 5 tenants, plus Sam the cat and Sam the dog, living in 2 rooms. The counselors were always locked out, not aware of the new tenants; and no one was ever at home when any of us went there.

Then came a terrible scare! We heard that Chris was hanging around with drug dealers and had been seen in several bars with them. My son got a call telling him the name of a bar where a friend had seen Chris with his new friends. By the time my son got there, Chris was gone. Next we heard that Chris had moved out of the cottage and had moved in with drug dealers. His landlord said he knew nothing about Chris moving out. The counselors had not realized there had been a move either. My sons got together and drove around until they finally found the house they had heard that Chris moved to.

Their plan was to knock on the door and ask for Chris, hoping to then talk him out of there quietly and quickly, leaving an unsaid message for his new friends to stay out of Chris's life.

When they arrived, they woke everyone with their knocking. They were let in and told that Chris was sleeping upstairs in his room. While one of my sons went upstairs to get Chris, the others went into the kitchen and began warning a young man to stay away from Chris. At that point, the person who had informed my sons where Chris was and had accompanied them, picked up an iron frying pan and began beating the drug dealer over the head. My sons apprehended him and were warning him to leave when someone said the police had already been called, so the frying-pan beater ran out and drove away on his motorcycle. My sons took Chris quickly out the back door and left.

From the fears Chris then expressed about these people, we hoped he might have learned the dangers in befriending people he didn't know at all.

He became more and more unhappy living in the small cottage.

"They might come back," he worried aloud.

He decided that what he needed was an apartment with a dishwasher. He wanted to buy new furniture and a vacuum cleaner. He also told his brothers he wanted to meet a girl with a car, so he wouldn't have to always ride the busses. His counselors decided they could probably accomplish one of his wishes: the apartment with dishwasher and furnishings, with earnings from his job.

He told us he wanted an apartment near a grocery store, a laundromat, and a church, as well as a bus stop; pressuring his case manager and job coach to help him find such a place.

Finally an apartment was found, and Chris's brothers and sisters contributed new furnishings. He had to leave his animals behind because pets were not allowed. One sister, Rosemary, took Sam the dog, until she could find another home for him. Her husband provided the pickup truck for moving Chris's belongings from the cottage, and agreed to go back and haul away the articles that were being disposed of. When he went to move the old bureau, he was shocked to find several kittens in the top drawer. He and Rosemary took Sam and one kitten, while the landlord took the remaining kittens. Chris had not told anyone about the kittens living in the drawer, and he never asked about them. At a later date, though, he seemed very relieved to hear that the animals were with his sister and the landlord.

When Chris was a small child, a doctor had told my husband and me that he would develop enough to have the skills of a third grader. When he saw how that information upset us, he reminded us of how much a third grader can accomplish.

"A third grader can answer the phone as well as dial numbers."

We thought about that.

"A third grader can prepare some meals and get himself a drink of water and food from the refrigerator, as well as know where foods are kept in cabinets."

We agreed with that.

"Some third graders do their own laundry and keep their rooms clean."

This was true, as we could see with our other children.

"Third graders dress themselves, groom themselves, and are responsible for personal hygiene, with some encouragement. A third grader can actually follow directions and perform independently sometimes."

When we left that doctor's office, we were more optimistic than when he first told us Chris would probably accomplish the level of a third grader, and remain at that level all of his life.

Now reflecting on that prediction, I was reminded of our original struggles with it, and tried to visualize a third grader in Chris's shoes, making the choices he was making, confronting the issues he had been dealing with Was he a third grader in an adult body?

CHAPTER 6.

Hurting Hands

"WHAT HAPPENED TO your hands?"

Frank had gone to visit Chris at his restaurant job and noticed that his hands appeared to be badly infected.

"They hurt, Frank."

The fingernails were peeling off; the skin around the nails was red, irritated, and peeling. Frank got him dismissed from work and drove directly to the doctor's office, where the physician diagnosed the infection as most probably caused by the chemicals in the soap at the restaurant. He couldn't believe that Chris had not been supplied with gloves to wear as a dishwasher. He considered performing surgery, but decided it would be way too traumatic for Chris. The recovery would present the possibility of further infection, and no use of his hands would be possible for several weeks. He decided, therefore, that it would be wiser to go the course of medicine. He prescribed a strong antibiotic and rest at home.

After a week, Chris's hands didn't look much better, and he was worried about missing work. The doctor conducted blood tests, which indeed showed that the chemicals had caused the infection. He prescribed a much stronger antibiotic.

During the second week off from work, Chris became irritable and worried about losing his job. His boss called him one morning and insisted that he come to work immediately. He caught the bus and was working in the kitchen when his brother, Frank, found him.

Frank questioned the kitchen manager about Chris being called in while he was on medical leave, and why he was still not supplied with gloves to wear.

"They're on order," the manager mumbled.

Frank reminded him that Chris had a doctor's excuse in their files and was not to be working with the infection caused by not wearing gloves while working.

"Well, why'd he come in if he wasn't supposed to?" the manager responded.

Frank clenched his fists and as patiently as possible, explained, "He's so afraid of losing his job; that's why. You know that, and you're taking advantage of it."

As Chris's hands worsened, were cracked and bleeding, the doctor insisted that he would never release him to the job unless gloves were supplied.

The first person Chris blamed was his job coach. She told him she couldn't understand what he was so upset about. She had, at the same time as this incident, helped Chris to open his own checking account at a local bank. It wasn't long before she had discovered that he had bounced 12 checks without her knowledge, and then wouldn't tell her who he had written them to. She was stunned to think he had written checks without asking her permission first. The blow to Chris was hearing that he not only had to pay all the check charges where he had bounced the checks, but had to pay the bank charges as well. So much for a checking account. He was very angry with the job coach.

From his chemically caused hand infection, he learned about Workmen's Compensation, and how to apply for it (with his brothers' help), to cover his lost wages. The restaurant had its own disability plan, and called in an expert to disclaim their liability; but their insurance representative actually agreed that Chris's hands had been infected by the chemicals in the soap, and he should have been provided with gloves from the start. Frank tried to help Chris to be more vocal about the way he had been treated, and to express his disappointments to his job coach.

His anger kept growing, and one day he refused to open the door of his home to the job coach. He screamed through an open window at her, blaming her for all his problems. She reflected to me, later, that it had been one year, as far as she knew, since he had adequately expressed anger.

"Yes!" she reported, "He's using much better communication skills, both regarding the job and his personal relationships."

He received a check for lost wages from Workmen's Compensation, which covered all the weeks he had been unable to work. At the same time, the restaurant personnel ceased being friendly or helpful to Chris, and denied that his infection had been caused by their soap.

Before Chris was ready to return to work, the restaurant notified him that he was laid off. The reason the restaurant gave for firing Chris was that he had not been a good employee after all. He was very hurt when the Job Coach explained that, but after a few weeks Chris shrugged his shoulders and told me he would be meeting with his counselors and job coach to talk about finding a new job.

CHAPTER 7.

The Accident

"Emergency!

ARRIVING AT WORK, FRANK WAS met by his supervisor, frantically informing him there had been a phone call about Chris being hit by a truck while crossing the street. Running back out the shop door, Frank shouted over his shoulder that he was going to the hospital.

Rushing into the emergency room, he was met by nurses who quickly ushered him into the cubicle where Chris appeared to be in shock and pain. When he tried to talk, his answers were slurred and not comprehensible. Frank leaned over him to comfort him, assuring that he would be all right. Chris moaned. His eyes were wide and frightened looking. A doctor urgently beckoned for Frank to leave Chris and follow him to another room.

Several nurses and technicians were attending to Chris as Frank turned and hurried into the hall, wondering what news the physician had to give to him privately. He saw the room the doctor entered and he ensued. Once there, the doctor immediately expressed his concerns about the possibility that Chris may have suffered some serious injuries in the accident. He pointed to a chair for Frank to sit in, as he sat down in another, appearing to be nervous.

"I can't understand him at all," said the doctor while blinking his eyes rapidly.

"This could be more serious than it appears."

He ran his hand through his gray hair. He then stopped talking, removed his glasses and rubbed his eyes several times before putting them back on. He took a deep breath, looked into Frank's eyes intently as he broke the news.

"I'm afraid he may have suffered some brain damage."

He leaned tensely towards Frank, trying to break this news as gently as possible. There was a long pause as Frank sat back on the chair, letting out a deep sigh. considering how he would respond to the nervous physician.

"Well," he spoke slowly, "you know that he was brain damaged before the accident, don't you?"

The doctor kept blinking and looking at Frank.

"Since his birth," added Frank.

Sighing a deep sigh of relief, the doctor seemed to sink into his chair. He carefully chose his words: "You mean that your brother was, ahhh, handicapped before being struck by the truck today?"

My son nodded his head, and the discussion then continued in a much more relaxed atmosphere. A few days in the hospital for

Chris to be observed and treated, the two agreed, would also allow him time to recover emotionally. There were some injuries to his leg and arm as well as a closed head injury.

The accident had been extremely traumatic for Chris, who couldn't remember what had happened. As our family visited him, we each tried to explain that the bright morning sun had blinded the driver of a pickup truck as Chris had been crossing the street. Chris had been thrown off his feet and up on to the hood of the truck before falling to the pavement. He did remember the driver cradling him in his lap until the ambulance arrived, but he couldn't recall the ride in the ambulance.

Chris gradually recovered during the next six months, undergoing outpatient physical therapy and medication. His memory was somewhat affected, and his knee was permanently damaged. We found out the driver's insurance would cover the medical expenses. Chris was left with a fear of crossing streets, and an increased awareness of the importance of using crossing lights.

"This is not going by without some legal action," Chris's brother, Paul, insisted. "I'll take care of this myself. I'll get copies of the police reports and I'll get a lawyer to help Chris. It's time the poor guy gets something for all he goes through."

Paul took care of the legal matters over the following months, assuring Chris he would get some money for all the pain he was having from the accident. Paul drove him to all of his doctor's appointments and physical therapy appointments, learning the extent of the injuries and the prognosis. Chris wore a leg brace for several months and was afraid to cross any streets. As he slowly recovered, Paul explained to him that it appeared he would be receiving some money for what he had been through. Chris expressed sympathy for the driver and didn't want to take his money. Paul was able to help him understand how insurance worked, and that the money wouldn't come out of the man's pocket.

Chris gradually began walking to the laundromat and grocery store again, resuming his independence and confidence. Loneliness still plagued him, although he insisted he liked having his own apartment and taking care of himself. We, of his family, called him and visited him daily. He often seemed depressed.

"I don't want a job coach any more," he told me during this time of recuperation.

That surprised me, although I quickly realized it shouldn't have.

"I don't want any more counselors," he added with certainty. "I don't want to be in the program any more."

I responded honestly, "I don't blame you, Chris. I allowed him to disenroll from the program he had been part of. He seemed to be relieved about that. I knew it was a big decision for him. It was sad.

In the following weeks, he sometimes didn't answer his phone or his door. Whenever this happened, I would hang a bag of goodies on his doorknob. An hour or so later, he would always call to thank me, and I would breathe a sigh of relief, knowing he was o.k.

Chapter 8.

The Attack

"MOM, CHRIS ISN'T answering his door."

My son, Paul, called me early one morning.

"I keep knocking, but there's no answer. The bag you left for him is still hanging on the door. When did you leave it?"

I replied that I had left it the night before. When Chris hadn't called, I suspected he had gone to bed early as he often did.

"I'm going back over there," Paul said. "I'll call you when I find out what's going on."

Paul went back and pounded on the door and called to Chris several times. Then he forced the door open. What he saw sickened and shocked him. It was heart wrenching and repulsive.

The stench of garbage overcame him as he entered the dimly lit apartment. Chris was cowering in a corner, trembling and frightened. His eyeglasses lay smashed on the floor near him as he crouched against the wall. He was covered with mayonnaise, mustard, spaghetti sauce, and other foods. He reeked of the odor of urine. His face was bruised and swollen, and his shirt was ripped.

Paul gently helped him up, asking, "Chris, what happened? What happened here, Buddy?"

Chris began sobbing.

"They broke in here and did this."

He clung to Paul as he trembled and cried, "Yesterday."

"They pissed on me and threw food all over me," he blurted out.

Paul sat him down on a chair and looked around. The refrigerator had been emptied. Its door hung open with its contents squashed into the waterbed, which had been slashed several times. All of Chris's paperwork (receipts, bills, old greeting cards) were shredded and strewn all over the floor, which was soaked with water. The garbage had been scattered on the water-soaked old carpet, causing a terrible smell. Family photographs lay, ripped into small pieces, all around. There were stains splattered on the walls.

"They took my hearing aids and my Social Security check," sobbed Chris.

"They took your check?" Paul was experiencing sadness mixed with rage.

"Yup," Chris responded, as he appeared to experience a chill.

His recliner had been totally slashed, and the TV lay broken and overturned on the floor, glass and parts scattered. Ripped from the wall, the phone was smashed to pieces.

Chris was totally traumatized and exhausted. He didn't want Paul to call the police for fear they would think he did something bad. Paul assured him the police were their friends and would come to help. He called them on his cell phone while consoling Chris. He also called me and told me Chris was fine, and he'd get back to me. (At that time he didn't tell me anything about the attack.)

Two officers arrived quickly, and upon entering they were immediately shaken by what they saw. As they examined the apartment, Paul explained what Chris had told him; adding that Chris was a good person who was learning to live independently.

"I don't know who did this," Paul said.

"I found him hiding in the corner still scared."

"Who in the world could have done this?" the policeman asked, horrified.

Suddenly, Chris blurted out that it was two boys from the neighborhood who had threatened him previously if he didn't give them money. He knew their names and where they lived. Their ages were 11 and 13.

Chris was able to lead the policemen and Paul to the home of one of the boys; a large old Victorian house, badly in need of repairs and upkeep. The boy's father stated that his son had not left the house at all the previous day. Chris got excited and shouted that the man was lying.

"He did it!" he accused, pointing at the red-haired young boy; but the father kept denying that his son had left the house. The officers responded that there would be an investigation, and the officers left with Paul and Chris. Paul took Chris home to his house for a few days, calling me when they got there, to tell me what had happened.

The police investigation eventually proved that Chris had been correct about the two boys who had attacked him. They were arrested and placed in a juvenile facility, ordered through the court system to pay restitution over a period of many months. A Victims Assistance Program also helped Chris to recover.

Each member of our family had different emotions to deal with as a result of this horrible attack on their brother. There was confusion and disbelief, sadness, discouragement and disillusionment, resentment and anger, sometimes experienced all at one time. We suffered with him and for him, while knowing at the same time that we would have to be forgiving. The ages of the boys helped in that requirement.

Chris's brothers and sisters repainted his little apartment and refurnished it. His sister, Donna, got him an alarm to wear that worked like a beeper. She programmed her phone number into it, so that Chris could beep her if he was in danger. At the same time, a loud alarm would sound from the mechanism he wore, to frighten off the attacker. She spoke to his neighbors in the adjoining apartments and asked them to call us if they noticed anything unusual around Chris's apartment. Paul installed a new door with double locks, and we bought a phone to replace the damaged one. We all worked on rebuilding Chris's confidence and trust.

Nevertheless, he suffered sleepless nights and lingering fears, even though he knew the boys who had assaulted him were in a juvenile detention facility. He told us he didn't like living alone any more.

Frank, in the meantime, had been going through a divorce. After a few months of considering it, the two brothers decided they would try being roommates again. Our family felt we had exhausted our efforts to help Chris live independently. It was evident that we could never let him live alone again. We felt sad having to make that decision for him.

Frank soon went hunting for a good house for them to share, as Chris began to show signs of interest and hopefulness about the new living arrangements planned. They found an old house in the city, built in 1890, which was close to a bus stop and stores. Structurally strong, it had an interesting history and unlimited opportunities for restoration. They moved in and began scraping off old layers of wallpaper, tearing up layers of carpeting, and shoveling debris out of the dark neglected rooms. Outside, they uncovered brick walkways that had been hidden by overgrown weeds. They dug up the yard and planted flowers, put up a clothesline where they each hung their clothes to dry, and knocked down old sheds and lean-tos. Evenings, Frank taught Chris how to play poker, and let him walk to nearby fast food restaurants.

Frank fixed Chris's room first. The walls had to be replastered and painted, as well as the ceiling. Of course, the layers of wallpaper and paint had to be scraped off first. The floors needed carpeting removed, and the wood floor refinished. Once the room was finished, Chris got new furniture and bedding, picked out new blinds for the windows, and a new rug.

They soon discovered the overwhelming problems though: the need for updating all the wiring and light fixtures, as well as a desperate need to replace all the plumbing and outside water pipes. They spent much of their time renting snakes and other tools to clear the pipes of tree roots. They were often unable to use the bathroom because the pipes were plugged up.

"Frank! No water!" became a too-often call from the bathroom. He couldn't hear Frank's responses because, well, he couldn't hear him through the door. For all of his life, Chris had depended on reading others' lips, even though he wore hearing aids.

I went by one day and found both Frank and Chris painting the garage. Chris was painting large areas, while Frank stood on a ladder, painting the trim and more difficult spots. Their clothes were hanging to dry on the clothesline, and the flowers they had planted were in full bloom.

"Time to water the flowers," Frank called to Chris as they painted. Chris put his paintbrush down and went into the house.

"Where'd he go?" Frank asked me, surprised to see him leave.

I pointed to the door of house just as Chris came back out with a glass of water for Frank. Frank came down the ladder.

Thanking Chris, he shrugged his shoulders and smiled at me. After drinking the glass of water he picked up the hose and handed it to Chris, while pointing at the flowers needing water.

"Oh! I'll water the flowers," Chris agreed, as he walked toward the waterspout on the side of the house.

"I guess he thought I asked for a glass of water," Frank commented as he climbed back up the ladder.

CHAPTER 9.

Writing On The Wall

"GET YOUR CRAYONS AND MAKE a picture on the wall."

"Go ahead, draw some nice pictures on the wall," Frank suggested to his young son, Frankie, who had come to spend the weekend with his Dad.

Frankie looked uncertainly at Frank.

"Go ahead. It's o.k." Frank smiled and handed Frankie a box of crayons.

Frankie looked from the box of crayons in his hands to the wall, and back again to the crayons. Then he looked back up at his Dad, with a slight smile.

"Go ahead," Frank encouraged. "You won't get in trouble. Have fun!"

Frankie took a black crayon slowly from the box, put the box down on the floor and, after looking back at his father for approval once more, very gradually began to draw on the wall. Before long he was having a wonderful time, drawing all sorts of pictures on the wall, with many bright colors; as his Dad sat watching and encouraging. Chris gradually picked up a red crayon and glanced at Frank.

"Go ahead, Harry!" (A family nickname for Chris) "Do your thing!" Chris added his writing to the wall.

All the children who came to visit Frank and Chris were invited to draw on the walls. Even some grownups left their drawings there. At Christmastime they drew Christmas trees and ornaments on the wall.

During the summer, when the city's parades passed in front of the house, many friends and family members joined Frank and Chris to watch from their porch. On national holidays, Chris made sure he was up early to help Frank hang out their large American flag. Chris was also using the city busses to visit a handicapped friend of his once a week, feeling very independent knowing how to change busses in the terminal.

Frank was working at a group home for adolescents who had developmental disabilities. He was a counselor as well as a teacher's aide in the school they attended. He felt drawn to the most challenged teenagers, and seemed to have a gift for helping them feel comfortable and to make progress. He was often overwhelmed by the paperwork involved for each day, and saddened when the time came as, one by one, the clients turned 21, and there was no place for them to move to. This particular program didn't allow for them to reside there after the age of 21. They most often had to relocate to distant cities where there were facilities for them, leaving behind all that had become familiar and comfortable. It was always quite traumatic, and often caused regression for these individuals.

At the same time, Chris had been accepted as a volunteer in a large nursing home, operated by an order of nuns who showed great compassion for Chris. A city bus, which transports handicapped adults, transported him. He waited eagerly to be taken to the facility on his volunteer days. He excitedly woke up early on those mornings and showered and dressed without any prompting from Frank. He hurried to finish his breakfast and be waiting outside long before the bus was due to pick him up. He wore his volunteer nametag proudly, and entered the nursing home happily greeting everyone he passed on the way to his assigned supervisor. He wheeled patients in their wheelchairs to therapy, meals, and recreational events. He ran errands and spent time visiting some of the bedridden patients. Everyone welcomed him and accepted him in a most loving way. He attended daily mass with them, and ate in the dining room with the nuns and nurses. He was given awards for his volunteer hours, which he excitedly framed and hung at home.

About that time, through a handicapped friend, Chris discovered that he could get money for aluminum cans when he turned them in at the local grocery store. He began going through the neighborhood looking for cans behind stores and restaurants, etc., and used the money from them for purchasing Christmas gifts for his nieces and nephews. I worried about him doing this but, on the other hand, saw the bending and walking as his only exercise, therefore probably beneficial to him. So Frank bought him a pair of heavy gloves to protect his hands, and we allowed him to collect cans. It was like an important mission to him, and occupied much of his spare time. Someone donated a can crusher to him, and he excitedly filled trash bags as Christmas drew near, when his sister, Rosemary, would come with her pickup truck to haul the bags of crushed cans to the grocery store. After turning them in for cash, she and Chris would go Christmas shopping.

Physically, though, Chris's problems began to increase. His feet, legs, and back hurt more than they ever had. Often his hands seemed not able to function as well as in the past, with increased loss of strength in them. He was hospitalized with pneumonia twice, and had to be on oxygen for a while at home.

The second time he had pneumonia, he was hospitalized for five days before going home with oxygen to be used all the time until he completely recovered. He seemed totally discouraged and depressed, no matter how much everyone visited and tried to cheer him up. He was weak and sometimes, lethargic. Frank looked after him and controlled his oxygen, as instructed by the visiting nurses who came by each day. Nothing seemed to help him get well. He wasn't even interested in watching TV or playing his hand-held computer games. We were trying everything we could think of to cheer him up, but nothing was working.

One day a greeting card arrived in the mail while I was visiting Chris. As he opened it and saw that all the nuns from the nursing home where he volunteered had signed it, he grew interested. The nurses and other members of the staff had also signed, and the card was full. I offered to read their comments to Chris, and he leaned forward on his chair to listen.

"Hurry back, Chris!" "We miss you!" "Get well! We need you!" "The patients are waiting for you to come back."

As I read the greetings they had written, I could actually see the color returning to Chris's face. He straightened up and listened as I continued.

"Sorry you're sick. Hurry back." "Hope you feel better soon. We miss you." "Get well, Chris. We need your help." "We're praying for you."

He suddenly stood up and turned toward me, adjusting the oxygen apparatus.

"I have to get better, Mom. They need me."

His determination to recover finally brought him back to health quickly. It was the greetings of the nursing home staff that gave him the desire to recover. He understood that he was really needed. It was only one week until he was able to go without oxygen, and by the end of another week, he was taking walks and asking when he would be able to return to the nursing home, because "they need me."

It was such a happy occasion when he was able to resume his volunteer work! He came home very tired, but extremely happy.

As our city's population grew rapidly, traffic increased drastically right in front of the house. Crossing the streets became more difficult for Chris. There were more and more strangers walking through the neighborhood; and noticeably less friendliness and acceptance.

After 3 years in the house, Frank and Chris began to think about moving to the mountains nearby. The plumbing problems plagued them and were beyond their financial limits to repair. The old house had more and more needs. Their brother, Mike, grew enthusiastic and hopeful that they would move to the mountains and be closer to him and his family, and to Paul and his family. He encouraged Frank and Chris to consider the move, and assured them he would be searching for a house for them. In the meantime, their sister, Rosemary, wanted them to move to the prairie where she and her husband resided, and assured them that she too would be looking for a suitable home for them there.

So the search was on, as Frank and Chris wondered where and when to move from the city, which seemed hotter and hotter each summer. We did worry about Chris not feeling independent any more if he weren't able to ride the busses and walk to fast food restaurants. We all agreed, however, that we would be sure he was always able to attend his favorite social activities with the group he had been a member of for 10 years, Faith and Light.

We included Chris in our discussions about moving from the city, but he didn't respond. We asked his opinion, but he shrugged his shoulders most of the time, making us uncertain about his reaction to a move.

The only time Chris showed enthusiasm about moving was when Frank suggested they buy an old motor home and drive around the country all the time. They joked about living wherever they wanted, for however long they wanted.

"We could visit everybody," Chris decided.

"We could park on the beach and watch the girls!" Frank suggested.

"O.k.," Chris laughed. "Let's go!"

CHAPTER 10.

A New Mailbox

"IT'S PERFECT!" FRANK EXCLAIMED as we drove down the driveway to an old trailer, in need of paint. It was on property bordering Pike National Forest. Frank, Mike, and I had been driven to it by a local realtor whom Mike knew.

"Chris will love it!" Frank said as he stepped out of the car into the brisk morning air.

"The furniture all goes with the place," the realtor proudly pointed out, as he unlocked the front door, and we entered to be surprised by the renovations inside.

"You're kidding!" Frank replied as he went from room to room, outside, back inside, checking out the bathroom.

Mike was following him, asking repeatedly, "What do you think?"

"Frank, what do you think?"

Frank walked around the property, talking about the possibilities of building a garage and an addition to the trailer.

"Hey! I could have a summer camp here! I could have a camp for kids who have developmental disabilities!" He eagerly dreamed as he walked behind the trailer.

"Chris could be my assistant!" He visualized while watching some birds feeding from the feeder as a breeze sighed through the trees. He and Chris already shared an interest in bird watching.

Bird Word

I heard a bird lay an egg today.
> *Couldn't see her but knew by what she had to say.*
> *Her voice changed briefly, not to one of pain.*
> *More like surprise at what had come her way.*
> *To me this seemed a little strange,*
> *having watched her prepare for this coming day.*
> *I think that even nature is amazed at Mother Nature's way.*

Frank John Montesano 2002

"Chris would love this place!"

The realtor suggested we get back in the car and take a look at the neighborhood. So we rode with him on the dirt roads, up and down the hills, past several lakes, and stopped at a large pond where a family of geese strutted across the road and into the water.

"Chris likes to fish," Frank commented.

"He could walk down here and go fishing."

Across the highway we could see many cows on a small ranch.

"That's where your mailbox would be," the realtor suggested, "right on this side of the highway, opposite all those cows."

Frank, Mike, and I agreed this place in the forest seemed right, but Frank would have to bring Chris to visit before making a final decision. We wondered how he would feel about living so far from stores, busses, fast-food restaurants, next-door neighbors, and the nursing home where he had volunteered for 2 years.

A few days later, Frank drove Chris up to the mountains to take a look at the "house in the woods" as Chris called it. Once there, they spent time walking around and hiking a bit in the forest. Chris kept saying, "It's good, Frank!"

They sat together on the front deck and talked about living there. Chris said he wanted to move there. Frank told him they should think about it for a few days. He wanted to give Chris time to consider moving out of the city, and maybe present some reasons why it wouldn't be a good idea.

The following day a woman from our church offered me the computer system her husband was no longer using. They wondered if Chris could learn to use a computer. When I presented the idea to Frank he got excited about it. He thought he might be able to teach Chris some things to do on it. So Frank, Chris, and I drove to their house to get the computer. We were very surprised to see the excellent condition of the equipment. Both my sons eagerly put everything in the car as my friends expressed their happiness at being able to help. As we pulled out of their driveway, Frank laughed, "Mom! I can't believe these people gave us all this great equipment!"

Chris reminded Frank that he had to get to his Faith and Light meeting in one hour.

"We're having a pizza party!" he exclaimed.

"I'll tell them about our new computer."

Faith and Light, an international ecumenical movement which supports persons with developmental disabilities, as well as their families and friends, had become a second family for Chris. Together they share, celebrate, pray in confidence and comfort, and renew hope. It's where they know they will always experience unconditional love and acceptance. The adults who direct this particular Faith and Light community have contributed greatly to Chris's recovery from hurtful incidents in his life, and to his personal healing and growth. He has always trusted them and loves them dearly. All of the volunteers in this organization have given of themselves to make Chris and his friends feel loved and appreciated. I see that they understand and practice the philosophy expressed by Mary McAleese of Ireland, on the L'arche Ireland website. *"We (modern society) have built our communities around the strong when in fact we should be building our communities around the weak."* Chris goes off on retreats and short trips with these people, who provide him with the opportunity to relax and be happy with his friends.

So he went to his meeting and told them about the new computer system and the possibility that he might be able to use it. He was excited as he announced that he and Frank would be moving to the mountains.

It was a few months before Frank and Chris actually moved. It didn't take them long to get settled. Chris had become overweight through the years and often breathed very heavily after walking or lifting. When Frank told me that Chris had started walking over a mile each day to get the mail, I wasn't sure it was a good idea. He had trouble with his feet, and he'd be all by himself on that lonely dirt road. I thought of all the reasons the walk to the mailbox wouldn't be a good idea. Frank assured me that Chris wouldn't go to get the mail if he didn't want to. It is, indeed, the highlight of his day, especially if there is mail for him.

Six months later Chris no longer breathed heavily. He had taken off 30 pounds by walking to the mailbox every day, his daily mission. Everyone began complimenting him on how good he looked, and he invited us to take the mail walk with him. We would all be huffing and puffing up and down the hills while Chris walked easily along at a brisk pace.

He needed new clothes after losing weight, so his sister, Patti, took him shopping. Patti has a knack for buying him clothes that are stylish and attractive, and he loves going on shopping trips with her. It's always fun.

As Frank learned to design websites, Chris worked at puzzles to glaze and mount for hanging. Patti bought him many 1,000-piece puzzles, which he completed very quickly. For many years Chris had been putting puzzles together at amazing speed, faster than most adults.

Frank was disappointed with Chris's inability to learn much on the computer. Chris, however, was satisfied to have his own email address, and participate in sending out ecards for holidays and birthdays. However, with daily persistence and encouragement, he learned to play some simple computer games, and often goes to his computer to enjoy himself

Fishing at the pond became especially rewarding when Chris's younger brother, Jimmy, brought his children along. Chris seemed to feel a bit fatherly around this brother, 8 years younger than he. He proudly responded to Jimmy's children when they talked to "Uncle Chris." Delighted when his youngest nephew, Joey, drew him a picture, Chris told about it to everyone he met. His nieces and nephews are very dear to him. He looks forward all year long to the day when he and his sister, Rosemary, cash in the aluminum cans he has collected, to buy Christmas gifts for each one. After moving to the mountains, the cans came from many people who collected them for him.

Now, it's always a joy for me to drive up and find Frank and Chris working in their yard: building rock walls, moving dirt, planting, etc. They wear bandanas tied around their heads as they push the wheelbarrow, climb the hills looking for rocks, and shovel dirt to be moved. Frank calls out directions which are sometimes ignored by Chris because he can't hear well, but they each appear to be happy.

They've watched many deer and elk in their yard and the forest adjoining it, listened to coyotes howling in the night, and stood together watching eagles circling in the sky.

One morning, Frank heard a lot of noise outside, and looked out to see a large bear getting into the trash. He and Chris went out on to the deck, apprehensively.

"HEY! GET OUTA HERE!" Frank yelled.

The bear turned to face him with a large pizza box stuck on its nose, and lumbered, defiantly, toward Frank and Chris, while trying to shake the box off. The two quickly turned and ran into the house, stumbling over each other, as Frank called over his shoulder,

"Never mind! We'll get outa here!"

They ran inside and locked the door, laughing and shouting. The bear eventually left, and returned a few more times before disappearing.

Once they were convinced the bear had left the area, they returned to their yard work. Although the work can be heavy and burdensome, Frank is always aware of Chris's limitations and doesn't let him work beyond his abilities. Chris never really complains although his doctor told me he's always in pain from arthritis and scoliosis. He just keeps going, until Frank calls for a break.

Watching Chris, I am often reminded of a verse associated with the Faith and Light organization:

"What is weak by human reckoning is what God has chosen." (1Cor.1: 27)

CHAPTER 11.

Special Education

CHRIS'S 45TH BIRTHDAY IS APPROACHING, and I've been reflecting on some comments once made to me regarding my pregnancy before Chris's difficult birth.

"Medical professionals should just let nature take its course. When you were in the emergency room in danger of losing Chris in your 7th month of pregnancy, they should not have prevented his probable loss of life. They should have allowed nature to take its course."

No! I thank God that we were able to save Chris's life! It is his life that has taught us the value of all life. It is from that pregnancy and birth that I also learned that God doesn't make deals, because during my pregnancy I had offered God this boy as a priest if only he would be born healthy; that's how I intended to show my appreciation for God's fulfilling my plan for Chris's life. Little did I know that God had a very special plan for him, and consequently, for me too. I learned what it really means to pray, *"Thy will be done."*

I was given a son who led me to my own priesthood, to which I am called throughout both the Old and New Testaments; and through the waters of Baptism. Chris led me into a much deeper relationship with God, teaching me about humility and faith, and the meaning of courage. I am the one who received a Special Education.

This son of mine loves absolutely unconditionally, both inside our family and outside. There is no one whom Chris does not fully accept and love. When even a dog sounds as though it sneezed, Chris offers, "God bless you." Most of all, he loves himself. He finally has accepted himself just as he is. He no longer expresses unattainable dreams and goals. He knows what makes him happy and what he wants to avoid.

He deeply loves children, and they love to be with him. They seem to always understand each other.

He gets excited about helping Frank to hang out the American flag, about new flowers blooming in his yard, the birds coming to eat the birdseed and cherries he sets out for them, and walking a mile on the dirt road to the mailbox every day; talking to neighbors along the way. The sight of deer walking nearby excites him, as well as family and friends (especially children) coming to visit him at his mountain home. He loves to watch the snow falling, to hold a newborn baby, to celebrate birthdays, and to see the moon and stars. He enjoys sporting events on TV, and sitting back to watch a good movie. He appreciates a rainbow as well as the rain. Comfortable with simplicity, Chris's inner peace seems to be the result of letting go of unrealistic goals and past efforts to attain the unattainable. In the letting go, he seemed more peaceful.

He has a spiritual sense, which is strong and faithful. He's very serious about praying. Praying is a very important part of his daily life.

I realize that this current state of happiness for Chris may be temporary, as other times have been. It is the longest period of peace and joy we have experienced with him. It is a time when we watch extreme patience and unconditional love drawn from Frank in caring for his brother. They have their differences, their arguments, and frustrations. It may not be a way of life for both men that will always be, but for now it is working. It is a relationship of respect and dignity, acceptance and remarkable brotherly love.

Chris keeps busy at puzzles, and has been making them into gifts. His brother, Mike, brought him some wood to use for mounting the puzzles, and Frank taught him how to use a small handsaw. Of course, I don't like to know when he's sawing because I'm afraid he'll cut himself. The edges aren't perfectly straight, but he's very proud of these "originals" he makes. I've got mine hanging in my kitchen.

Recently, at their home, Chris asked Frank and me to help him moved a completed puzzle on to a piece of wood he had cut. We had to slide the large puzzle off the table on to the wood.

Chris held the wood as we slowly and painstakingly moved the puzzle slowly toward the wood. Suddenly, the puzzle broke apart and fell all over the floor. Frank let out a shout, throwing his arms up in the air, while I gasped, "Oh, no!"

"Damn!" Frank tried to grab the falling pieces.

"Oh, no!" "Oh, no!" is all I could repeat over and over. I quickly tried to prevent the puzzle from any further falling apart, but as I did I caused more of the puzzle pieces to fall off the table.

Chris burst out laughing! He put the wood down and began picking up the puzzle pieces, as he continued laughing.

"It's o.k." he said, gulping from laughing so hard.
We helped him pick the pieces up quietly, while he kept laughing. Then Frank walked out on to the deck, and I followed, as Chris began putting the puzzle back together.

"I can't believe he's laughing," I remarked to Frank.

"If that were me, I would be devastated."

Frank nodded and said, "I know. I know. He's a real lesson, isn't he?"

"Makes me think," Frank reflected, smiling.

A few months ago, Chris was given the opportunity, at a Faith and Light meeting, to string beads into necklaces. It was amazing how quickly he caught on to it, and how much fun he had choosing the multiple colors for each necklace. He even took some materials home and made more to give as gifts at the next meeting. Seeing his success with that, I asked him if he would be interested in making Rosary Beads to be donated to the poor of the world. His eyes lit up as he agreed to take on this new project. I assured him I would get in touch with a lady at our church who supervises that work.

I met with my friend, who brought along the beads, string, and crosses to be made into Rosary Beads. She instructed me how to make all the tiny knots along the way, dividing the beads numerically as they should be, so I could teach Chris how to do it. I discovered it wasn't as easy as I thought it would be, and found it difficult to make the tiny knots with the string. Expressing my doubts about Chris being able to tie the tiny knots, my friend asked that we give him a chance. So I took the materials to Chris who told me he would start making Rosary Beads for the poor right away. He was excited about this new endeavor, anxious to make them for poor people. What a gift to The Church!

When I left, he was sitting at the kitchen table in the trailer, leaning forward intently, as he began stringing the beads. The door was open because it was a warm day. We had all said, "Good-bye," and I went through the doorway, looking back to see Chris working intently on the Rosary Beads, as Frank turned on the computer at his desk.

℘ ℘ ℘

There's a place in the mountains
Where we hear the trees grow
Buds burst into flowers
Snowflakes falling on snow

We hear the clouds floating
New dawn startles me
And the voice of creation
Is as clear as can be

O! Lord of the mountains
We hear your words
In the sound of the wind
In the song of the birds

In the soul of the mountains
Where God answered prayer
Where welcome abounds
And life's finally fair

Where we carried our burdens
And gave God our fears
Where happiness happened
And joy fills our tears

O! Lord of the mountains
What love we have found!
Your child is now happy
On this holy ground.

Following is a postscript, which comes from a conversation I had with Chris. I had explained that his brothers and sisters had contributed reflections for this book, and asked him if he would like to do the same. He was enthusiastic in his agreeing. He was very thoughtful, serious, and reflective, as he calmly took his time before each comment. He understands that I will write everything just as he expressed himself. I hope you'll enjoy him as much as I did.

Pat

POSTSCRIPT

Chris's Reflections

About family and friends.........

About My Dad...

My Dad was a very good man. He was a hard working man. He had his own business!

When he was a milkman, a long time ago, he let me go on the milk route with him, and he let me help. That was fun!

When I went to school in Boston, Dad let me bring my best friend, Billy Saks, home to New York to visit us. Billy said he had a good time.

Dad taught me how to clean washing machines in our laundry room in New York. He was funny too.

My Brothers...

My brother, **Frank**, gives me so much help! He helps me pay the bills, and helps me do email and send cards to everyone on the computer. He taught me how to play cards, and he likes to plan things with me. He likes to talk about things with me and have good talks. He likes to go to Faith and Light with me, and he likes to plan things for Faith and Light. I want my friends to come and see where Frank lives with me, to come and see the water and the ducks.

*My brother, **Paul**, lets me help with laundry and cleaning up the trash. When it snowed he let me help him shovel the snow off the deck. One night he told me he loves me, and we drank pop together.*

__Mike__ gets my medicine for me. He helps me too. He takes me to the store sometimes. He lets me sleep at his house and clean his yard and rake the leaves. Sometimes he comes to visit and see my puzzles.

*My brother, **Jimmy**, is a hard worker! I understand he works very hard to get money for his kids. He thought I got mad at him once, but I never got mad at Jimmy. I thought it was funny when he pushed me down the hill on the carriage. I know he cares about me.*

My Sisters…

__Donna__ bought me lots of beads so I can make her a necklace. She wants me to make her Rosary Beads too. I hope she likes what I make for her!

*My sister, **Patti**, always lets me help her! When I washed her dishes, she said I did a good job. She likes the way I do her dishes. Sometimes I help her fold laundry, and she said I do that good too! She likes me to help her.*

__Rose__ is a good sister. She helps me a lot, and takes me to her house. I remember when I helped her move into her new house.

My Brothers-In-Law

Marty *likes me to come and visit. He knows I like sports, and he talks to me about sports.*

Aaron's *a good brother-in-law. He helps me with his truck when we take all the cans to the store for money.*
At Christmas time he helps me to get the money, and takes me shopping.

My Sisters-In-Law...

Dina *likes me to come and visit, and go out to lunch with her. She bought me a picture frame for pictures of my nephews too. She took me on a trip to visit her aunts and uncles and cousins, and we went to where Elvis used to live. He had a swimming pool in his back yard!*

My sister-in-law, **Terry**, *gives me puzzles to do, and brings food over to us. She lets me water her flowers too! I help her with her flowers.*

Siobhan *is a very nice person! One time she drove me home from the mailbox when she saw me there. I think that was a good thing for her to do.*

My Nephews...

Paulie *lets me do his laundry. He asks me to visit him and his wife, who is so nice.*

Michael *surprised me when he came to my Christmas play at Faith and Light!*

Daniel *always says 'hi' to me when he sees me! He let me do his laundry too.*

Marty *likes to play games. We get along very well. He showed me around their new house.*

Jonathon *is a nice person who always says 'hi'.*

Vinnie *likes sports very much! He likes to ride a bike too. He is always good to me.*

Edward *likes to play games. He likes his dirt bike, and he showed it to me and told me all about it.*

Jason *likes to visit us. One time he came to visit and he helped to cook the hamburgers and hot dogs.*

My nephew, **Frankie**? *Oh, man! He helps me so much! He hung my can crusher up on the wall! One time he drove me home in his new car!*

Joey *thinks about me a lot! One time I gave him a baseball hat to wear fishing, and he wore it! He drew a picture for me. He likes to play, and he thinks about me.*

My great-nephew, **Clay**, *likes to talk! He wants me to run with him, but I can't run fast enough.*
My Nieces...

Michelle *likes to talk to me on the phone. One time she gave me ham and cheese sandwiches! She gave me boxes of cereal too!*

DiAnna cooks for me. She likes me to go shopping with her too. She drives when we go.

Maria is a funny girl! She likes to laugh! Sometimes she helps too.

Meghan gave me a get-well card when I was in the hospital. She always likes to talk to me.

I remember **Nicki.** I haven't seen her in a long time, but I know she was always very kind and very nice.

About My Friends...

Tim! He is the one who told my Mom about Faith and Light, and he took me there. He always asks how I am and how my mother is.

Fr. Duane is a nice priest. He invited me to mass when we were celebrating my Mom's birthday, and he came to have dinner and birthday cake too. He always says 'Have a good time.' I pray for his mother every day, that she will be happy at her home.

John and Diane are good people! John is a very funny guy.

Fr. Tom sends me emails all about God and the world. He sends me pictures of the mountains, and he's helping my mom to find a job.

The Valdez Brothers are good boys. They like to go fishing. Andrew doesn't want to go home when he comes to visit. Timmy likes to walk to the mailbox with me. They came to Faith and Light with me.

__Ray__ likes to take me places! He likes to take me to Wendy's for dinner. He has fun with me. He's fun too.

__Margaret__ is a very good friend of mine. We talk a lot on the phone, and I see her at Faith and Light meetings. She's always friendly and nice.

About __God:__ I can give prayers to God, and He takes them. Then he gives help to all the people who need it.

About __The Fire:__ (The Hayman fire, burning near Chris's home as this book is prepared for print)
It's bad! I hope they get it out! I'll feed all the birds and animals who come out of the fire.

About __Life__: Life is good. I think life is good.

℘ ℘ ℘

I'm looking for love in its simplest form

Acceptance, respect

Where dignity's born

Where my life will find

The riches I seek

In gentle compassion

In the soul of the meek

Printed in the United States
1433100006B/232-249